NOTTAWA TWP. LIBRARY
BOX 398/112 S. CLARK ST.
CENTREVILLE, MI 49032-0398

SPIDERS SET II

DADDY LONGLEGS SPIDERS

Jill C. Wheeler
ABDO Publishing Company

visit us at
www.abdopub.com

Published by ABDO Publishing Company, 4940 Viking Drive, Edina, Minnesota 55435. Copyright © 2006 by Abdo Consulting Group, Inc. International copyrights reserved in all countries. No part of this book may be reproduced in any form without written permission from the publisher. The Checkerboard Library™ is a trademark and logo of ABDO Publishing Company.

Printed in the United States.

Cover Photo: Animals Animals
Interior Photos: Animals Animals pp. 5, 9, 10, 13, 17, 20, 21; Corbis p. 7; Fotosearch p. 15; Heather Proctor / Bio-DiTRL p. 19; University of Southern Queensland p. 11

Series Coordinator: Stephanie Hedlund
Editors: Heidi M. Dahmes, Stephanie Hedlund
Art Direction: Neil Klinepier

Special thanks to Mr. Ron Atkinson of the University of Southern Queensland for his help with this project.

Library of Congress Cataloging-in-Publication Data

Wheeler, Jill C., 1964-
   Daddy longlegs spiders / Jill C. Wheeler.
     p. cm. -- (Spiders. Set II)
   Includes index.
   ISBN 1-59679-293-0
   1. Pholcidae--Juvenile literature. I. Title.

QL458.42.P4W44 2005
595.4'4--dc22

                                                   2005042132

Contents

DADDY LONGLEGS SPIDERS 4
SIZES 6
SHAPES 8
COLORS 10
WHERE THEY LIVE 12
SENSES 14
DEFENSE 16
FOOD 18
BABIES 20
GLOSSARY 22
WEB SITES 23
INDEX 24

Daddy Longlegs Spiders

In the animal kingdom there is a phylum, or division, called Arthropoda. Members of this phylum are called arthropods. They have skeletons on the outside of their bodies. Many insects are arthropods, including the class called arachnids.

Mites, ticks, scorpions, and spiders are all arachnids. They have two body parts and eight legs. Spiders belong to the arachnid's **order** Araneae. There are more than 100 **families** in this order.

The Pholcidae family of spiders is called daddy longlegs. There are about 350 species of these spiders worldwide. Daddy longlegs are also called cellar spiders. That is because they are often found in basements.

Daddy longlegs spiders are often confused with another arachnid. Harvestmen are often called daddy longlegs, too. But, harvestmen are not true spiders. They have one-piece bodies and only two eyes. And, they do not produce **venom** or spin silk.

Humans have helped daddy longlegs spread all over the world. Many daddy longlegs hitched rides when humans moved from place to place.

Sizes

Daddy longlegs have bodies that are quite small. The body of a female daddy longlegs is only about 10/32 of an inch (8 mm) long. A male is even smaller. Its body is usually only about 8/32 of an inch (6 mm) long.

Even with these small bodies, daddy longlegs look quite large. Their legs can be up to 1.2 inches (3 cm) long. That is five to six times larger than their body! So, daddy longlegs are well named.

These tiny bodies and spindly legs make daddy longlegs spiders look delicate. But, they are good at taking care of themselves.

Opposite page: Several differences help people tell daddy longlegs apart from harvestmen. One is that harvestmen, such as this one, have a single, round body part.

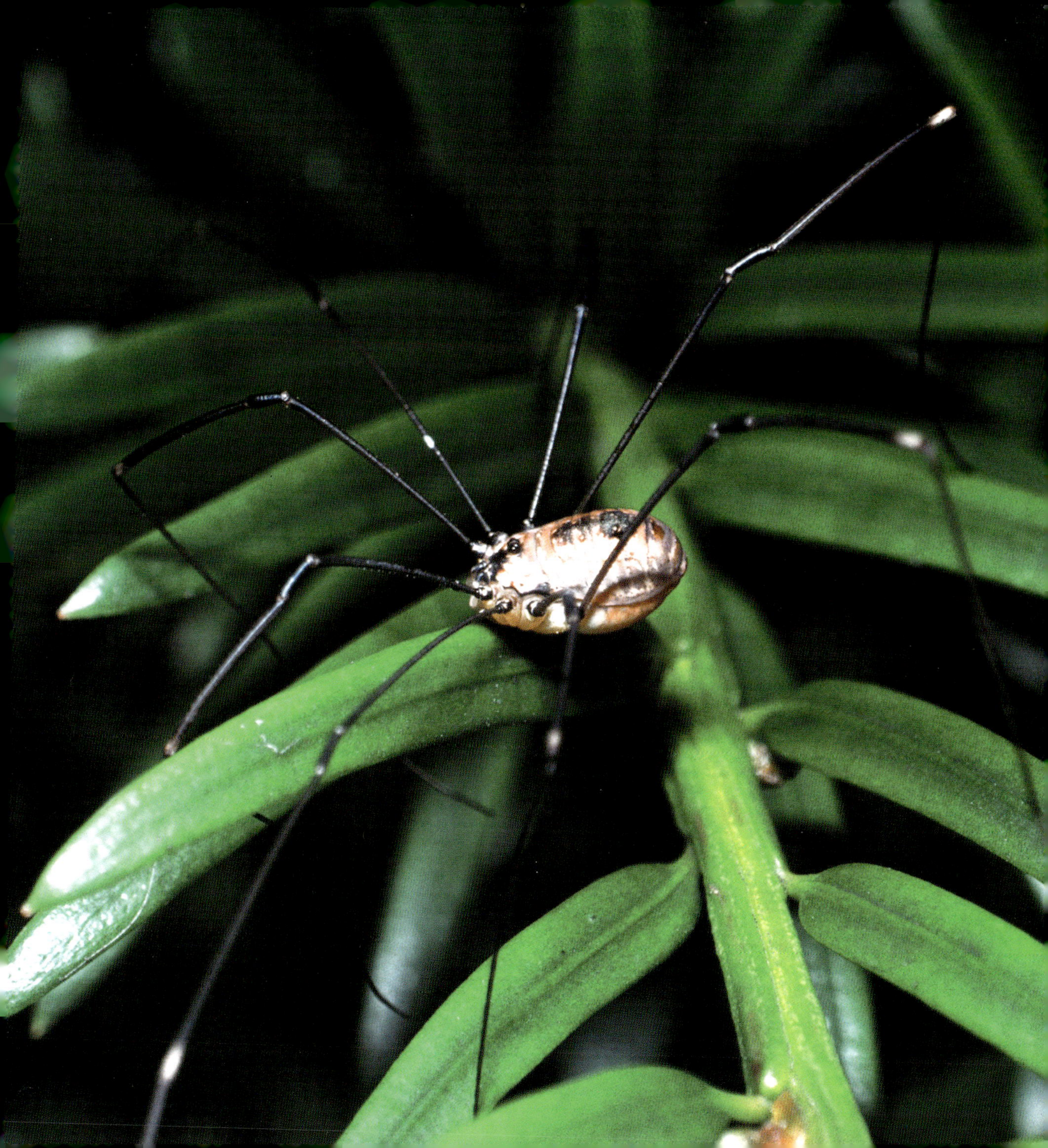

Shapes

The delicate look of daddy longlegs spiders may be because of their body shape. Daddy longlegs have two body parts, like all other spiders. The **cephalothorax** is the front body part. The rear body part is called the abdomen. It is usually **cylinder** shaped.

All spiders have eight legs. The legs of a daddy longlegs are attached to the cephalothorax. Daddy longlegs also have two **pedipalps**.

The pedipalps are located at the front of their cephalothorax. Spiders use their pedipalps to grab their prey. Male daddy longlegs use their pedipalps in mating, too.

Spiders also have two **chelicerae**. These leglike organs have fangs attached to them. Daddy longlegs have chelicerae, too. They use them to **inject** their **venom**.

The Body Parts of a Daddy Longlegs Spider

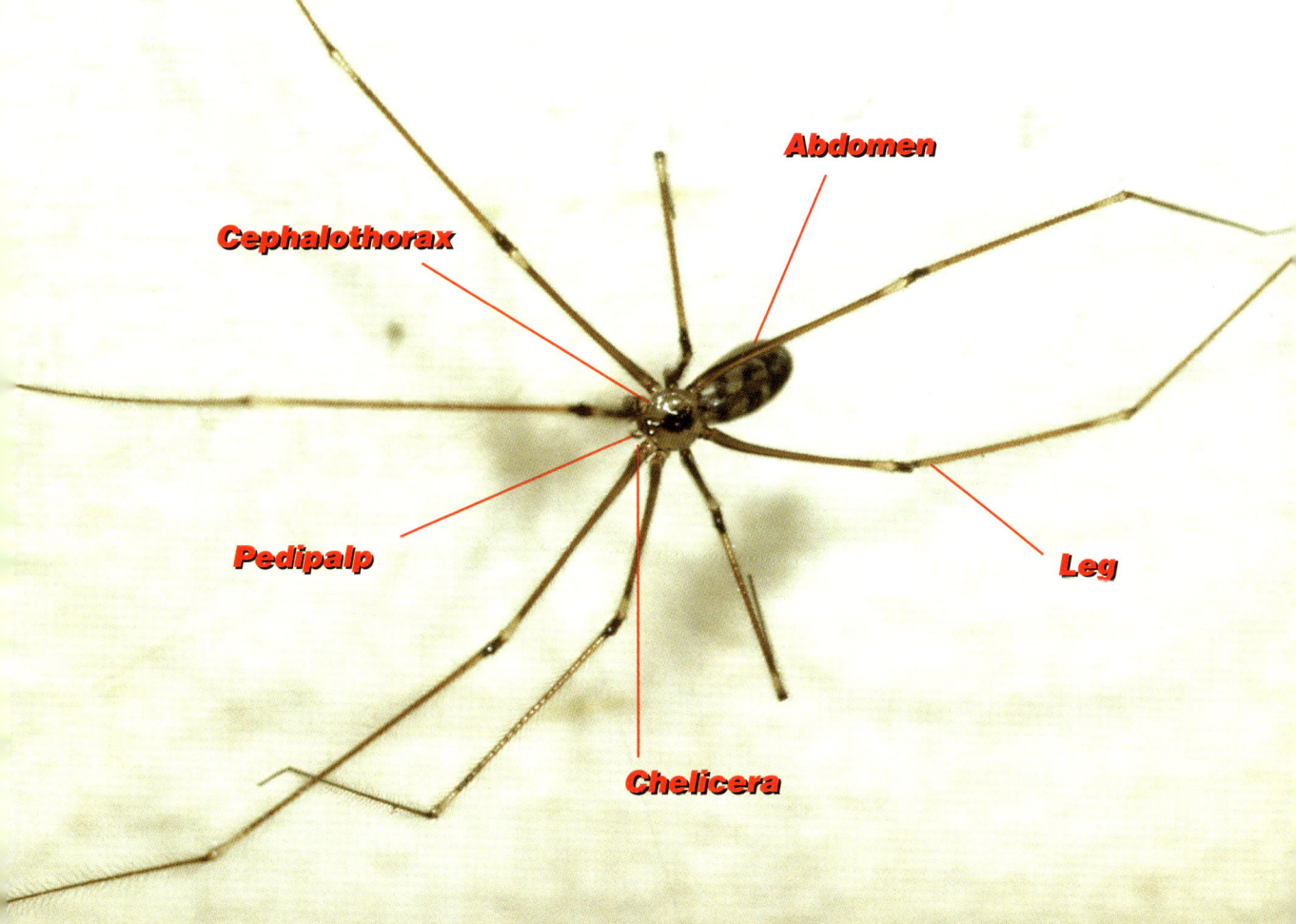

- Cephalothorax
- Abdomen
- Pedipalp
- Leg
- Chelicera

Colors

The body of a daddy longlegs is not very colorful. These spiders vary from light tan to greenish- or grayish-brown. You can almost see right through their delicate legs and bodies.

There is a popular myth about these pale spiders. The myth says that daddy longlegs spiders have the deadliest **venom** of all spiders. The myth is false.

Daddy longlegs spiders are so pale in color that the sun shines right through them.

Imagine you have a live daddy longlegs and a microscope. The spider is so delicate, you can see the blood moving through its body.

    Their **venom** is deadly to many bugs. Yet it is one of the weaker venoms in the spider kingdom. Plus, it would be very hard for a daddy longlegs to bite a human. Scientists believe its jaws are too small to get through human skin.

Where They Live

Daddy longlegs are pretty easy to find despite their drab coloring. They prefer tropical and **temperate** climates and dark, damp places. They like places with average temperatures above 64 degrees Fahrenheit (18°C).

Daddy longlegs are found in most countries around the world. They are most common in the British Isles, the United States, and Australia. Some live in basement corners. Others live outside under leaves or in caves.

These spiders prefer to live alone. They spin loose, messy webs that are about 12 inches (30 cm) wide. They spend most of their time hanging upside down in their webs.

Daddy longlegs are particular about their webs. They will abandon them if they are too dirty. They just go spin a different one somewhere else.

Scientists believe daddy longlegs live up to three years. This is longer than many other spiders. Many people believe their life span is so long because they are safer from **predators** inside. Plus, it never gets quite as cold in houses. So, the spiders are less likely to freeze.

The best time to see a spiderweb is when it is covered with frost or dew. Since daddy longlegs often live indoors, it is difficult to photograph their webs.

Senses

Daddy longlegs use their senses to stay alive. These spiders have six or eight eyes. The number of eyes depends on the species. In fact, some cave-dwelling species have no eyes at all!

Still, those daddy longlegs that do have eyes do not see very well. They rely on sensing vibrations instead. Vibrations are the best way for daddy longlegs to know a snack may be near.

A daddy longlegs's web is not very sticky. But, the daddy longlegs is very sensitive to the slightest movement. Sometimes a bug flys or crawls onto the web. This creates a vibration. The spider then runs out to grab its prey.

All spiders have hairs on their legs that sense vibration. The daddy longlegs spider attacks anything that causes these hairs to move.

DEFENSE

Daddy longlegs like to eat other spiders. But, other spiders also like to eat daddy longlegs. So do wasps, centipedes, reptiles, and shrews.

Daddy longlegs try to avoid their **predators** by staying hidden. This is their main defense against predators. One way they do this is by building their webs in dark corners. However, staying out of sight does not always work.

A daddy longlegs has another defense against predators. It may start to spin if it senses danger. It spins around and around as fast as it can. It soon looks like a blur.

This spinning seems to confuse the daddy longlegs's predator. It cannot tell where the spider is. You can test this yourself. With a stick or broom handle, touch a daddy longlegs's web with the spider in it. The spider may start to spin for you.

The life span of a daddy longlegs may be shortened for many reasons. A spider may starve, be eaten by a predator, or be caught in extreme temperatures.

Food

A daddy longlegs is a good addition to a home. It will eat lots of flies, mosquitoes, ants, and moths. The spider gets this food three ways.

Webs belonging to other spiders provide a daddy longlegs with food. The daddy longlegs may crawl into another web. Next, it creates vibration to draw the other spider closer. The daddy longlegs then attacks the spider and eats it.

The daddy longlegs may **raid** another spider's web when that spider is away. It eats whatever prey the other spider has stored for later.

A daddy longlegs also uses the vibrations of its own web to sense prey. Then it attacks the prey and quickly wraps it in silk. After it is wrapped, the daddy longlegs bites the prey. This **injects** its **venom** into the victim.

Once a daddy longlegs's victim is dead, the spider **injects** it with **digestive** juices. These juices turn the prey's insides to mush. The daddy longlegs then slowly sucks out the prey's insides.

Daddy longlegs have powerful sucking abilities. They can suck a fly dry through the tip of the fly's leg. It can take a whole day to suck a bug dry.

BABIES

Daddy longlegs need food in order to have energy to hunt and mate. After mating, a female daddy longlegs produces 15 to 20 eggs. She wraps each egg in a bundle of silk. Then, she carries the egg bundles around in her **mandibles**. This gives the eggs time to develop.

Baby spiders are called spiderlings. They hatch out of their eggs in two to three weeks. They

A daddy longlegs carrying spiderlings

spend their first few days riding around on their mother. Then, the spiderlings go their own way.

All spiders wrap their eggs in silk egg sacs. Some sacs contain a few eggs, but others have hundreds. A spider may leave its egg sac in a hidden location. Or, it will carry the eggs until they hatch.

Daddy longlegs babies molt like many other spiderlings. This means they shed their old outer skeleton for a new one. These little spiders shed their skeletons five times before they are mature.

GLOSSARY

cephalothorax (seh-fuh-luh-THAWR-aks) - the front body part of an arachnid that has the head and thorax.

chelicera (kih-LIH-suh-ruh) - either of the leglike organs of a spider that has a fang attached to it.

cylinder - a solid figure of two parallel circles bound by a curved surface. A soda can is an example of a cylinder.

digestive - of or relating to the breakdown of food into substances small enough for the body to absorb.

family - a group that scientists use to classify similar plants or animals. It ranks above a genus and below an order.

inject - to forcefully introduce a fluid into the body, usually with a needle or something sharp.

mandible (MAN-duh-buhl) - one of two grinding jaws found on many insects.

order - a group that scientists use to classify similar plants or animals. It ranks above a family and below a class.

pedipalp (PEH-duh-palp) - either of the leglike organs of a spider that are used to sense motion and catch prey.

predator - an animal that kills and eats other animals.

raid - a sudden attack.

temperate - having neither very hot nor very cold weather.

venom - a poison produced by some animals and insects. It usually enters a victim through a bite or sting.

WEB SITES

To learn more about daddy longlegs spiders, visit ABDO Publishing Company on the World Wide Web at **www.abdopub.com**. Web sites about these spiders are featured on our Book Links page. These links are routinely monitored and updated to provide the most current information available.

NOTTAWA TWP. LIBRARY
BOX 398/112 S. CLARK ST.
CENTREVILLE, MI 49032-0398

INDEX

A

abdomen 8
Araneae 4
arthropods 4
Australia 12

B

British Isles 12

C

cephalothorax 8
chelicerae 8
color 10, 12

D

defense 16

E

egg sac 20
eyes 14

F

families 4

food 8, 14, 16, 18, 19, 20

H

harvestmen 5
homes 4, 12, 13, 14, 16, 18
hunting 8, 20

L

legs 4, 6, 8, 10
life span 13

M

mandibles 20
mating 8, 20
mites 4
molting 21
myth 10

P

pedipalps 8
Pholcidae 4
predators 13, 16

S

scorpions 4
senses 14
silk 18, 20
size 6
skeletons 4, 21
species 4, 14
spiderlings 20, 21

T

ticks 4

U

United States 12

V

venom 8, 10, 11, 18
vibrations 14, 18

W

webs 12, 14, 16, 18